After June

After June

poems

CHARITY GINGERICH

GREEN WRITERS PRESS   *Brattleboro, Vermont*

Printed in the United States

10 9 8 7 6 5 4 3 2

Green Writers Press is a Vermont-based publisher whose mission is to spread a message of hope and renewal through the words and images we publish. Throughout, we will adhere to our commitment to preserving and protecting the natural resources of the earth. To that end, a percentage of our proceeds will be donated to environmental activist groups. Green Writers Press gratefully acknowledges support from individual donors, friends, and readers to help support the environment and our publishing initiative.

GReen
WRITeRS
p r e s s

Giving Voice to Writers & Artists Who Will Make the World a Better Place
Green Writers Press | Brattleboro, Vermont
www.greenwriterspress.com

ISBN: 978-1-7336534-2-8

COVER ART:
Michelle Kingdom, "Light as Dust," 2018.
Hand embroidery on linen, 10˝ x 13˝.

Contents

After June

Mountains, Sunset, Redbird, River:

In the catalogue of voices, there are fake dogs.

There is pitch and then there is tone. Pitch is *correctness*; tone is
    what you do with that.

Strike your best plates, the *we're all home for supper* vintage ones
    with brown-gold leaf,
                               and listen for laughter.

You must pay attention to rain, the most fundamental of
    instruments; trees-in-thunder jazz.

Of many voices—
               a violin and a swan
               the wind and a child,
               this lamentation—

few can touch what God must have heard
when the first strand of sea and the first breadth of sky separated.

Even now, when I am sure of little else, I am sure of harmony.
    I found my own voice by blending in

       with the women around me.

I haven't loved too many boys

Mostly I've really loved
the idea of love: a tall blond tenor
who between rehearsals once said
have a kiss, and offered
my seventeen-year-old self a chocolate.
This is specific but beside the point.
Later he soloed about a golden chariot
to heaven in that little hollow
at the end of the sloping aisle
of the church of my girlhood,
always filled with music. When it burned down,
all the songs I sang there became
an unfurling tapestry stitched with birds
whose flight spelled *help.*

The Thing That Music Leaves Me With

The first note of any song is about precision.
This, more than beauty, will carry it through.

My mother has always insisted on two necessities:
a glistening countertop and perfect pitch.

Both imply listening, as in *it is evening*,
then close harmony while washing up.

Even now when I open my mouth, searching
for the correct vowel shape, confidence

and knowledge always a little at odds,
beginning a song is like opening the right door
while carrying a candle, and the echo that follows.

I *Always Want to Look at Art This Way*

> At the Rhodes Art Gallery, Sisters of Loretto, KY

Here in the gallery of natural light, it is the hunger hour.
The crucifixion of Christ surrounds me in miniature

but for this great rood of burlap, resin and wood
alone on a hushed blue wall, an echo of Mary's robes.

—As if to soften the vulnerability and decay of the artist's eye.
There is no beauty here, yet I can't stand upright,

as though to be level with him as his flesh is eaten,
as it is being eaten, hands, feet and chest crumbling

until his body is too slight to cast a shadow—
makes me guilty, again, and blackhearted all over.

From another room a record of *Appalachian Spring* plays,
its rills and swells and robinsong a little too joyful

for this moment. My question had been "what repulses most?"
meaning the art, meaning I was not prepared.

Outside, a bird I can't place calls *where? where? where?*
and a bell rings—dinner, or another nun has passed over.

Little Cup of Stars

In German, the word for thirst is *durst*,
which sounds like the clearest of brooks. And *durste*,

a piece of Old English to dare, to venture, to presume. I dare
to have a big thirst, "to be allowed to be thirsty."

The body is a yellow house, with one room for every wish;
the heart an easy guess: morningstarness pulsing

like the Schuman arias I practiced fervently
but never got to perform, except for a friend on his deathbed.

Like any good vocalist, I gulp water daily, vigilant for dryness,
for any sort of losing out. I was taught that laziness = foolishness,

so that each note, each thought, each room of the body
is in need of constant cleansing. Not for what I can detect,

but for what I cannot. My thirst then a sort of bravery,
my house modeled after *kleinegroß*.

O God, if I were to shake you for a cup of stars,
how lost would I be in their richness, the milk

of my longing, their beauty, becoming this cloud-high roof of me.

Silver Dollar Sunset with Paper Doll

I came into my girl body fully in the sweet air and clinging heat of our winters in Sarasota with grandparents, who only went to the beach fully dressed, and under whose disapproving eyes my sister and I made the short dash in our bathing suits from bedroom to tiny kitchen to the yard hemmed by a wash line, some orange trees. My sister loved to sun, and I pretended to for approval, my body soft white and plump, prone to deep angry sunburns. I preferred the activeness of shelling, the white sands of Lido and Siesta Key thick with coquinas—or bean clams—conch, cockle and lightning whelk shells, the occasional sand dollar. Here I could forget my hand-me-down beach dress, too short, too tight, my knees and nose already pink from salt winds and sun. While my body sweated its way to shapes I did not understand, I borrowed a legal pad from grandpa, a newspaper man. I took very little interest in what he wrote, preferring my own heroines, who I dressed in my words much as I had dressed my paper dolls as a child. For years, I'd had to wear "practice dresses" my sister made for me as she learned to sew, itchy shapeless things cut from experimental fabric that reminded me of parlor couches, or a grandmother's ancient bathrobe. Once, on the last day of our visit, my grandfather took note of my scribbling, the fact that I stayed indoors mostly, my shells smelling up the kitchen. In his awkward, clownish way, he rewarded me with two silver dollars. Along with my shells, boiled fresh white and empty, I have kept these always, to remind myself that memory is like the whorl of a seashell, with its tiny staircase, rooms for the sea.

After June

Outside, *form* happens: field, fritillary, sky.

In the garden, tiny melons sweat,
sweet moons under the sun.
I want to be still like that again
under my best dream tree, barefoot,
you up there at the window, humming.
Making sure of things. Even the sky
wore an apron of stars.

Survival only seems possible
from this distance: recognition
and acceptance the heart's two faces.

Now—

I am a stubborn fort
with bluebird sentinels.
The sea is a long way off.

Why Taking Notes on Vermeer is really a Cover-up for—

In "The Music Lesson," Vermeer allows the woman's face in the mirror
to turn toward the man leaning close by, though not too close;
and outside the mirror, she in fact keeps her face intent on her hands
in that self-conscious way the admired have. *Reflected light, saturated light.*

But what is this really about? I'm sheepish to say I've been obsessed lately
with love stories not my own. *Clear light, light that draws you in,*
some focal point I'm only vaguely aware of but doggedly follow.
In the well-worn novel discovered in girlhood, and now rediscovered,

I've read the passage of the doctor and teacher on a horse—
just before she nearly dies of typhoid!—at least six times this week,
usually before going to sleep, and can't stop dreaming in dulcimer tones.
In my day/dreams, I always go back in time, never forward.

No one ever sat me down as a girl to tell me if this is odd. But really,
who would choose to kiss an extraterrestrial on the moon
when one could go back to the violet mountains and a red-haired violinist.
The vanishing point is the artist's ultimate weapon:
                                        the white pitcher
on the table leads us right back to the woman's sleeve—
is and is not the focus (only my coming to terms with longing)—
so crisp, I can hear it rustle as her fingers move over the keys.

Complaint, Comply, Compline—

Near Loretto/New Haven KY

I like the high, slightly wavering voiced monk best
bravely filling up the dusk—that creeping sandstorm

signaling a day's end—and though I don't know who he is
I know he too fears the fading light, the insufficiency of stars,

that he knows the mossy nest of a shadow's curve, *little death*,
and every note between dew and hunger. Meanwhile I

am too timid to climb into my soprano range in the shower,
a squeak between facial scrub and shampoo, a long white echo

down an immense hall, where the shapes of novitiates
can still be seen gliding along the walls at night. My song

a sunny buttercup-turned-owl, his, honey in the mouth
of a cave. On the drive home, all of Kentucky is shining gates

of a new spring, a landscape unfamiliar except in curves,
the quilted ache of longing that is each burst of daffodils.

How to Bear With It

In the graveyard of the Sisters of Loretto, KY

Lord, I would never sit on a bench away from the sunset,
or bathe my infant niece in a tea-cup.

You are so generous with majesty:
exultant blue-feathered-this, holy mountain-scape-that.
I don't know how to look away. Just now the sun's pressing close
to a cloud so it looks like the state of grace—or West Virginia.

The two most important questions in life are
how much is that star in the window, and,
have you followed the red fox to the field of longing.

I want to add something about my mother's copper-and-gold eyes,
like two small butterflies hovering in the raspberry bush,
something about forgiveness and *are these ripe yet?*

Thomas Merton wrote "to sing is to begin a sentence like *I want to get well.*"

I want to leave this place while the light still touches everything:
tombstones, spooky white angels, two fresh graves.

The obligation of human nature in miniature—

1.

> When the Asian ladybug lands
> against my windowpane, its body becomes a prayer bead,
> a quick prayer

2.

> moving upward in the sunshine of a hard tumble. Today
> I threw away a bouquet of flowers gathered in 1995
> from a wind-chapped mountain meadow

3.

> in Washington. *Out West*, as we called ourselves,
> my family, collecting shiny things of this earth; now, guilt
> is my go-to emotion. But the shelf of my special things

4.

> has held the sturdy star shapes of the child-
> loved blooms as long as I asked, so there's that.

> Why is it I can describe the world all day,
> and still not say how I feel?

5.

> *A pumpkin on the seashore is what kind of fish?* My niece asks
> over supper, over the everyday music of our lives,
> our knives and forks poised over what we understand: sustenance,

6.

        now; tonight, the moon. Aberglaube that little dragon
  folded on my teacup shelf: only as fragile as I would have it.
    Whatever puddle the heart makes is always the right one.

7.

            Your problem is, you have read books.
                 The sun will not be dictated to.
  This is what I imagine the lilac bush to say, the lilac bush

8.

  that is really my grandfather. Planted before he died young,
        my first recollection of spring, of gathering up
                   and being gathered.

The Afterlife of Lepidoptera

The heart by definition is an agrarian tapestry
with an up-welling brook at its center,
hedges of forsythia, chickens, room for violets.
To believe otherwise is to bolt the fence
in the pasture behind you where the moonlight ends
and the farmer's prize bull begins;
the heart dies a little every day for lack of tending.

Let's get back to the business
of milkweed and thistle, joe-pye weed and clover;
when have you last caught a Diana fritillary,
Beloria bellona, black swallowtail or painted lady
for the sheer joy of its wings,
for the experience of learning how they work,
the webs and scales of their flying jewel bodies
in the meadows between two farms—when have you last
stood in such a place, *stood still*, and not
merely thought of standing there, paper doll
with her paper moon on a backdrop of imaginary
happiness.

Listen, the snow is falling. White roses
filling the air. I believe this is a reminder—
that when death comes it will be our longest moment
of suspension. The air we swim through
thick with the pieces-of-us, not as brokenness
but as an invitation to finally stop;   we'll build a butterfly,
as if it were a house we could finally live in.

Every Stargazer Knows Her Vowels

The white duck floating downstream in the long light

is facing a bridge, is facing a treeline, is facing a small boat.

Not quite on the other side, a flock of starlings flies across

a weathered brick façade, whose name is *evening nest.*

The girl in the boat is busy with an orange, thirsty.

She has been waiting for this light all her life, and now

it has come she thinks of her mother's best china,

how careful the children were not to chip it all those years.

Soon the river will be filled with small, glinting pieces,

and the moon, hanging like a postcard in the sky:

dear child, come home. The table is set, and we are ready to sing.

The History of Words is Not the History of Sound—

Awake, I take myself to every blue hill
I've known, or felt, or heard,
searching for sounds like *onward*—
a red fox and hummingbird moth both busy
in a field a *sea of bee-balm*—.

A nice dream is still a dream,
bewail, perhaps like *womanhood*, less a state of being
than an echo.

Who
would you share an apple with,
its inner star and health?
Every woman who wears orange
in a meadow knows:
she is not *form* but *idea*.

The history of words is not the history of sound but
confusion. After, birds stopped
singing a long while. An aisle formed in the meadow
called *whistle, whistle, wound, wound.*

If I'm not Praising—

For Michael, 1952-2009

Beauty is sometimes just recognition:
my mother's hands cleaning berries,
my father's voice, a Baroque trumpet on the phone.

And the sky, always some curve
of medieval pink or blue: I can't carry sadness just now,

between bodies, love narratives, and songs
with names like *Blazhen Muzh* and *Pasterzem mym Pan,*
my tongue a little stronger every day.

I've come to realize pitch is like a good treeline:
it surrounds but holds its distance.

I've sung so many *Amens* since your going,
how can a few more hurt this much?
Practice makes permanent, not perfect, you always said.

Hear how the breath catches over thirds, like stream-ripples
on stones. Blue cup mountain stream elixir *in place of,* not *because.*

Imagine How Much Beauty You Miss Everyday—

In January I am a prophetess of sunless browns.
There are no snowmen, and I miss the blinding fields of home.
Then on my walk, in this place that is only for passing by,
graceful hill, blue spruce, purple and yellow blooming cabbage.
And far off, the Mountain of Hope, gray-and-lavender
against its curve of sky. The memory of June never gaudier.

"My Noon, My Midnight, My Talk, My Song"

From Auden's "Funeral Blues"

A butterfly's laconic dip and upward swirl
from daylily to daylily is all the breeze we have today,
the felled redbird by the roadside so still, so perfect

in death, like art.   So *intact*. I want to believe
it was an accident:
                    two beautiful objects colliding

somewhere between a sky, soft as a silk scarf,
and a blue spruce filling the air with its pungency.
There is something like grace in looking

without expectation, without judgment: stillness
upon color, color upon stillness.
                    Our light, our shadows

leave impressions in the dust: blue water in red canyons.
I have not yet lost she who is my east and west,
my everything. But I have passed moonflowers

spreading secrets at dusk, and kept them until morning.
We are all of us dying of one sorrow or another.

I've sung all the hymns as proof.

I'm All Prayed Up

> ". . . Like a moth that tries to enter the bright eye"
> —Johnny Cash, "The Mercy Seat"

It's morning again, and again I'm alive to sing a little of it.
I've watched the sun climb the side of a pink house, some trees,
scuttling just now like lonely brooms across their mother's kitchen
floor, the sky. It's spring again, everything playing dead,
no color for miles but a train whistle, a muskrat washing its face
in the river on my walk. I want to stay in this view indefinitely,
perhaps in the hope of seeing as if for the first time—
the pileated woodpecker's soft knocking, as if hesitant to wake the trees,
the exact moment the redbud comes into itself, a timid flame
spirit, and the river, always the river, dark and dreadful on top
but filled with freckle-tipped, orange, red and blue crayfish burrowed
and burrowing in the cracks of rocks. The life of the river is here,
rushed over, unnoticed except by those who hunt and study, watch.
How to not take all this for granted, left swaddled up in words
as incense, our tired prayers. I want to put on a headlamp at nightfall
and go down to the river to watch winged, finned and clawed things
stitch up the dusk, to say I've been witness to something more than
beginning and ending.

Landscape after Rain

In the blue-green mist the goldfinch

is folded against the spruce, like a love-letter.

I am packing, leaving this mountain

for a new view. Or so I tell myself.

How does one say goodbye to wisteria,

the holler with its birds and frogs and wild mint?

You must not ever stop being whimsical,

Mary Oliver says. What else is happiness, then,

but the ability to see a pond, some ducks and a tree.

My precious things are mostly packed, and I think of home:

what is home, but sweet marrow

of our earliest recollections, that deep ache?

I can move because I know this,

I can move on, because I carry this.

Appalachian Postcard from a Midwest Girl

At the end of Monongalia Street (and my new home) is a mountain
    and a curve—
then houses in colorful layers,

> at center one of tea-rose yellow
> a long way down.

To think I could fall into this deep garden
of rock and wisteria in the simple act of *home-going,*

> a wrong turn and—gables::
> catch me brambles;

the sunset beckons and stands still,
yet, these days, night cannot come too soon,

> the moon a badge of longing
> where my heart should be.

Venus and Jupiter, most visible just after nightfall
a reason to look up, *stay safe.*

This is all to say: I remain uprooted in these close hills, but for you
and the Virginia bluebells, which were early, like a sign.

Somewhere, loneliness is a pond missing the face of a deer as it drinks.
Think of that, and paint its picture.

Three-Sister Houses in Winter

Wilson Avenue, historic South Park, Morgantown, WV

Pink sister house is the hooker on the street, her porch missing like virtue, or front teeth. In the white froth of January, I can feel her shudder, her bones fragile as she gathers herself together against another winter. In the 1910 postcard she is one of three, identical down to the filigree above her windows, at the peak of her roof, like a father's careful signature. A coal-baron father who built three houses side-by-side for his three daughters at the turn of the century. Only their paint is different: sister house one a shout-out green greener than a perfect lawn, or envy, sister house two of palest yellow—that *just enough* yellow, first light of morning on a tree, a girl's hair; and sister house three, now just a home-away-from-home, blazing pink, like the lips of a burned-out coquette. My Serbian roommate has taught me the art of sighing, me and the house, and we spin our sighs into a cocoon of longing, into magical draperies for the original windows, those wide eyes that are her one beauty. Day after day, I press my fingers to the thin glass, afraid I may discover we really are lost rabbits in a cave, that the beauty of the landscape beyond is merely endlessness. I want to make a promise to this lost girl, to my roommate who has survived a war, that come spring I'll recover her flowerbeds, coax up the fresh faces of snowdrops and grape hyacinth to warm her dainty feet. Every day, coming home over the river, the white sycamore—then as now—stands over it like a giant candelabra, unlit but waiting, always waiting.

Conflict is the Only Way to Intimacy

There must be a cry before there can be an echo:
You understand *help* better than *blackberries*,
your body wired for thorns, poison, attack.
If we let your voice out in the rain, it would come back red tulips.

•

The woman has been very careful about collapsing her body,
the act of folding delicate, discrete.
She goes from a bridge with vines, and birds rummaging in trees
to something you could pocket easily: a polished bone, a small cup.

Landscape in winter, imagining what is there, trying on joy—
the red maple drops her pocket handkerchiefs,
and because trees are too large to carry
from the countryside to the city, taking up watercolors is wise.

This familiarity with yellowish skies could be prophecy, or hope.

She wants a shed of light in these close green hills has a potent fold/ripple effect,
and you, cupping your ear to catch each ringing note.

•

She is *yes* to you. Think about it. Put a finger in the wound
and think shape: land, maybe, or Blue Bunting: entry and exit.
This isn't metaphor, but longing, which is natural.

That Evening Light I Love

Between knee-high meadow and mountain curve,
after dinner, the first watermelon of the summer cleaved, eaten,
I pull off the road suddenly to see the poppy-gold sun
slant just so in the trees, your hair, all that up ahead-ness.

And in the barn the new filly, soft brown as you'd expect, nurses
then nibbles our fingers, like teething, with salt.

A friend asked recently if I can write when God seems distant.
What do we mean by distance, I wondered, the artist's brushstroke
pausing between *intention* and *desire*, perhaps peonies
in the garden, heavy with scent and light and bees.
We are as close to God as our intellect will allow, or,
as close as the nearest object/tive that inspires us to love.

Oh dusk already, and mountain laurel a little rusty in its blooming.

There's a Black Cat in My Garden

I think he thinks he belongs to me, his yellow eyes

like two lanterns in a coal mine there in the petunias.

Even after I've fed him, he trips me all the way down

our sunken staircase this side of Hunger Mountain.

My great-aunt is dying, after 97 years of determination.

All sharp angles and good grammar, her world a classroom,

her going is one more untethering of the tent.

My youth and its gospel meetings and cornfield tag.

In the new neighborhood there's a good hill,

the heart waving its Midwestern flag in my eyes. Once atop

I forget to look back, but retracing my steps it is very

dear wind-hover, this is your blue ridge speaking.

This is what happens when you think of *what could be.*

Walking, with Blackberries

There's nothing like walking in June in an aching body, discovering
    blackberries.
Like a fox swallowed by brush they hide, but light finds them out,
no less lovely for their wild abandonment in a burned out lot, my
    greedy hands reaching, reaching.
If you insert the tongue just so there's a surprising end to *looking* and
    grasping:
seeds tiny as sand, soft as new calf chin fuzz. The tongue, perplexed,
    withdraws,
but always wanders back for more: a question never answered quite
    like *this.*

Doorways

Every day with you is a treasure hunt:
acorn gnome top hats, old red and blue factory glass, fossils
and feathers. When I kiss you, I am searching for seashells,
like the faint purple Coquinas I found on Lido beach as a girl.

Tonight, hemstitch of fireflies threading the dusk
with their small-winged longing. You explain that the females
hover lower over the grass than males, their protectors,
who must be quick with their light. I stood in every doorway
of delight. Like a silver smear
the moon came up over the trees and we walked a little while.

Landscape with Passenger Train and Lunch

I don't know what the weather's been like.
Outside, things happen: a little autumn, a little squirrel-joy.
Inside, I crave all beautiful moments
even as I pick up your prescription, listen to you yell about your keys,
my missteps, your hurt. Enough to fill a mountain, or a train.
We climb aboard one on Saturday as planned.
The Cheat Mountain Salamander, promised to *take you through*
some of the wildest mountain wilderness you will ever experience.
And though the hills through our window have lost their summer glow,
inside our green car with its snug little seats
we are the deer beneath the yellow maples at their peak,
sustained for winter, twining, following an instinctive track.

Beauty is a Mountain We See when Driving Our Car:

These days there is very little landscape,
just curve, curve and—oh my, Christmas.

I am unprepared for any magic but that of mountain ranges,
blue and still and wordless, coming and going
in the fog. My heart is ringing its little bell
waiting for something greater than help, help, and echo.
Is there a language that contains another silence,
one shaped and deepened by the word? Elie Wiesel asked,
but of course he had a right to.

More and more, sadness needs its own special shelf.
But I am determined to keep mine prettily decorated:
see the snapshot of Mt. St. Helen's? I slept once in its shadow.
We all thought it dead, and it showed us.

Let's Not be Abstract about This

Yellow butterfly under sun-bleached, curly-limbed sycamore
by the pond with its silver-headed sunning turtles,
please take a message to Mary, white and still
out there at the center, her head bowed to the world:

> Mary, can't you see
> I don't have a boat
> and am doubtful
> even at this distance
> of how your sorrow
> makes the moon more
> every night beautiful
> in its black lace sky.

At the National Aquarium, Baltimore

Of course I wanted to see the *invasion of the jellies:*
oceans out of balance display. But red and green paddle boats

shaped like dragons and full of kids circled in the harbor,
and I wanted to escape. "The green one with the gold eye, please."

Even love a little bruised will stay you: a sort of rootedness.

So we crowded around glass cases—
strawberry-picking days of my girlhood.
Claustrophobia will do that.

You took every photo I asked for, with fierce care.

They looked like dollops of summer preserves
left to elongate and grow legs and lace underwater,
multiplying, like beauty left without a predator will do.

I Said, "Just So You Know, The Holy Spirit is Intimidating Here"

At the Rhodes Art Gallery, Sisters of Loretto, KY

We'd rented a cabin called Joy in the woods; mid June,
a week of birding, looking at the world, rest for two poet-girls.
We hung our work on clothesline like laundry, made lists
for the historian nun on duty, one that ran something like this—

1. Slave oblates?

2. Honking in the woods about 9:30 by the lake—deer or frog?

3. Where is the path to the little trees? (As in: seedlings.)

Surrounded by meadow, trees, lake, sky, we discovered *what's
    a heaven for.*
Took notes from mother phoebe, her nest above our porch light,
as she snatched bugs from the underbrush; snapped a photo
of her three birdlings, their mouths tiny orange trumpets of
    supplication.
We stood in the meadow at the end of the longest day of the year
to see if the moon was *really something*. It wore the sky like a silk
    nightgown.

On the steps of the art gallery, my memory of the Holy Spirit
sculpture was actually "Angel of Mercy," copper and smoke,
its "face" biblically terrible, Pharaoh-like, as if about to cough up
    frogs.

Or was that my heart: painting-in-the-making. In June, in and out
    of
a cabin in the woods, in and out of ear-shot of the phoebes' baby-
    hymns,
the Holy Spirit took me by one hand, the Angel of Mercy by the
    other.
I'd like to think we played in the wind under the white sycamore.

Landscape with Girl and _____ in a Forest

We followed loose rocks and moss to the stream bed
looking for the raccoon's tree, finding an 'ostrich' tree instead,

with a burl so big its spine curved as if in *running pose.*

Isn't love about forgetting all else for its sake?

Let's paint, I said, meaning winter,

as in, let's fortify ourselves with landscape;

how nearly landscape spells escape seems no accident.

I like light on my trees, I said as the forest thickened.

The difficulty is all in finding the right light:

a tree is a pilgrim is a bear is a fire is an outstretched hand.

"In the heart of every man and every woman a kind of
Garden of Eden endures, where there is no war, no
death, where wild animals and deer live together in
peace."

—Irene Nemirovsky, *Suit Francaise*

The twilight is even more beautiful than we could have imagined,

like two fawns standing at the edge of an open field, star-soft, a
little dazed.

What could go on and on does; so that to remember daylight seems
unnecessary

instead of impossible. The girl with the hope-root is waiting to
plant,

because death is like eating a certain honey, is like this path of
Queen Anne's Lace,

which is the only clothing anybody needs anywhere. So your
nakedness

isn't nakedness, the sky a blue dress folding itself again and again.

Two Fawns in a Winding Lane—

In September the wind chimes toll like prayers
for the newly dead, brown sparrows flying up in haste

from late roses along the sidewalks, like laundered hearts.
The lace curtains of the living are always drawn here.

I am rounding a bend in a street called Lila, a little wild
in my longing for reprieve from—you name it,

and in a stranger's garden, two fawns are twined in feeding
like a 1960's plastic garden statue; we all blink, but there is little fear.

Only when I speak do they move, soft brown smudges
nibbling pachysandra furtively, soon arching away
over hedges. I could follow them home.

Of all the houses far from home I've haunted—

I've most loved Pink Sister House on the corner of *oak shot through*
  with light

and a brick house with a sleeve of roses the color of maidenblood rising

                                                    to its curlicued roof.

I've learned I'm easily charmed; a window here, a window there.

Last night the mountains looked like cutouts of themselves,

strips of construction paper torn to enact *ripple* and *line.*   A heart scrawled

just anywhere is still a heart.   At this stage I'm only guessing,

the right move and all that; on one of my last morning walks here, beguiled
  by fog,

a redbird landed on a low wall with a backdrop of yellow irises.

                                                    That

seemed as good as anything.

Benedic Anima

Today I will praise you though I cannot sing loudly about it.
Today I will praise you through this window—
my disappointment, the blue jay bullying
all the small brown winter birds to other birdfeeders—.
Today I will praise you I couldn't afford the best seeds.
Today I will praise you for this holy restlessness.
Today I will praise you for this timid unhappiness.
Today I will praise you, mother shepherdess, for that spring
& its friendly white peacocks and rusty warm earth.
Today I will praise you for love, though love is not
all I feel, or need, or trust, lashing pines in February wind.
Today I will praise you, please I need a virgin mirror,
in which no reflection of *that girl* remains, her witless beauty.

From the Country of Ordinary Sorrow

Lunches in June: remember how we ate wild
blackberries like farmers of a boundless harvest:
asparagus for detail, rosemary-and-honey chicken

for practicality—lace moon the picnic cloth we flung
in any good meadow. If hope is a horse in winter,

how many roads should we take?
We tried bringing seasonal bouquets to the table,
the flames of forsythia a sort of hearth

for roasting apples: first, child's play, then
the sort of play children make who are desperate
to *hold on*. As a girl I dreamed the world was shaped

like an endless field one simply had to walk across,
that it could fit into any well-kept kitchen like a piece of fruit.

All the stuff of pirates next to mountain, mountain laurel; or,
leaving West Virginia

There's nothing special about the dresser you and I haul

down two flights of steps, but a ladybug lights on a drawer

                              as if to bless a hidden treasure.

"All of a sudden it hits you—all the things you don't need. And I'm drinking
    lemonade here,"

Mom says, with hardly a pause, as if the one is indicative of the other.

        She is speaking of course about how to empty a three-story house

as though it were a jar of marbles,

so as not to burden the left-behind. I don't know what it says about me

that I've filled up the shells-of-places so easily, apartment after apartment,

                              made them home, mourn

a little at every dispersal, take a long last look at *that* fuchsia rhododendron,

the house on the street 'round the corner with a roof like a flying Dutchman.

These views are the knickknacks on my shelves, the tiny vase

on the mantle declaring *West Virginia, wild and wonderful.* The boy in the
    ocean blue shorts

in the painting over the mantle is front and center. He seems to know that
    when next I return

                                                       to this
                                                       state,

I'll be an almost-bride or a what-if girl. For now my golden lamps

and other loot are mostly packed, and I'm going home

to help my mother decide what *preparing your boat*, and *good weather*, means.

Walking to Merton's Hermitage

Twice I passed a sign, *Monastic area, do not enter*,
a Tuesday in March is as good as any day for a scolding,
and this path of limestone fragments lined with not much
as good as any path on which to drag a heavy heart.

But for my polka-dotted scarf, I could have been
one of the mute trees on either side of the path,
not brown or green or silver but *dirge* in any language.
Easy for *him* to write and live endlessly in contemplation;

he had no father or mother or siblings for most of his adult life
to love and meddle and pester him back to the world,
coax him away from the privilege of books and prayer,
of every shape the moon makes from May to January.

Cerulean who? Oh—another bird in another morning.
I finally crested the knoll and came 'round the bend
to see the squat dwelling of my latest hero, disassembled now
as wind chimes, an occasional outcry of daffodils,

the bit of pinkish rock I'd picked up on my way in.
Perched on the cement slab of porch next to my armor—
a bag of books + knickknacks of a girlish vagabond,
I stumbled off some prayers, cast forlorn looks at the cross,

and didn't think to answer when the wind chimes rang out
twice, very distinctly and simply as soon as I arrived,
though I heard their subsequent silence and thought, oh song,
oh welcome, then picked up a book on how to paint tears,

or how to refurbish a turn-of-the-century highchair,
something appropriately abstract and artsy to fill up
the hole that is spring, the hole that is robin chuckling
over his first worm, his sunrise breast everything-out-of-reach.

Window with Pink Geraniums and Aching Body—

My mother irons shirts
as though they are landscapes of the dead.

Meanwhile I pick at stitches to an old wound:
note: stumps in front yard need grinding, let's call it relationship,

black like the coal train's aching body
at the edge of a river filled with sunset. Today, things are

clearer but not easier. I think they call that *mercy*.
My life a tiny book I carry, trimmed in yellow wallpaper,

its words some mistake for smudges. I sang in a cathedral once
whose glass-stained windows turned the light to gumdrops

on its pillars—blobs of child-like delight, or whistled notes
of an artist, carrying her tools from one job to another.

On Choosing the first Ice Cream of Summer:

You mop your forehead with a rose, recommending its thorns
—From John Ashbery's "Hotel Lautréamont," Section 4

Listen: choose a field, one close to a shabby white shack, boasting
      six flavors that change daily: *white chocolate watermelon*
and so forth. You'll feel like you're in the middle of nowhere, because
   you are,
      a grown-up daughter and her parents, a few nieces
in mismatched flounces and starry head-gear the main attraction;
      oh wait—down the street is a red house
with a balcony where Lincoln once gave a speech. Imagine the sky
      as he saw it, all legs and black and rickety voice,
some little storm blown in to remember him by. Try to lick
      from the bottom up and trade cones, a nut here,
a cherry there. Don't take any pictures or try to make it memorable;
      a favorite teddy might fall face-first in mud,
the drive home be under a moon whose shirt is buttoned in rain.

May Elegy

For Aunt Sara

When death came, lilacs
were sun-heavy, swaying,
I was familiar. Part of *after*.
Still, dazed. All-of-a-sudden:
facts to sort, clothes
to choose; we couldn't bear
to say her name. She became *the body*.
The heart alone is astonished.
How do you carry a wounded bird
to safety? The orange trumpet
of its beak tense with warning.
Lord, you never told us this river
would come to break us, like blooms
from stems, from the crossing-over.

Heirlooms

In my childhood garden, the white roses
grandfather planted before I was born
unclench their small fists: bud after bud bending

low to the ground as in confession, a heady scent.
When I snip three, the thorns mean business, mean *remember*.

Inside, I've just put away the paper snowflakes,
our winter roses, in granny's medicine drawer, breathed
wintergreen and Union salves, incense of bygone prayers.

What most separates the dead from the living anyway—
a little more dying, a different kind of music.

How to say creature comforts *in winter*—

after Mary Oliver

Under an ice-blue sky
lives a red-brick house laced

all around in windows,
like the decorated captain

of winter long ago, demanding
a good view. I walk by with a lady

in my head: lady lady, what,
all in black again. And the trees,

long glittering shadows on the snow
with only the calligraphy of claws

and brittle nests to remember
the birds by. The idea of song

decadent, long-ago, pain
about good posture despite this stiffness

between the shoulder blades.
Back home, Mom in the bath says

she has a *technique* to keep warm
and keeps the curtains in the house pulled back

to avoid claustrophobia. And I think,
of course February is a chattering symphony

playing to awaken the fields of stars
come spring, daffodils, our inside-out scars.

Mom Swam on Christmas Day

At Lido Beach, Sarasota, FL

After fifty years of wading, she decided to get in for real. For the longest time she stood in the shoals, a tiger lily in a thrift-store-new bathing dress, the waves breaking hard, the Atlantic unfurling its hair like an anguished, warm-hearted widow. *The warmest December on record*, the locals repeated. Mom, Dad, my sister I, remnants of a whole family, beckoned again and again for her to join us where the waves lifted us effortlessly as flotsam, a chandelier here, a coral-crusted mirror there, *restoration art*, like that sold in the beachfront warehouses we'd wandered into. We scrounged for treasures with our toes: so many almost-perfect conch shells, little royal houseboats with no one home. When she came to us, we held her like an anchor as she floated, tentative but ready, saltwater and seagull air making her shriek like a girl, making us glad we'd let go of Christmas-as-Christmas, that glistening, lonesome holiday.

Artifacts

Mannequin

At six degrees above zero, her small breasts seem more frozen than usual, the ugly-but-cute *bears doing winter things* sweater she models for eBay like a loose map of the history of women. My mother turns her backwards while tightening the sweater's red buttons. Because: the men in our house, because: her instincts tell her *form* for form's sake is unnatural, must conform.

Matryoshka Doll

In a square with red geraniums in Warsaw, we choir girls shopped for pretty, strange things to put in our pockets. Naturally, we looked at nesting dolls, those perfectly painted ladies with a body for each secret. Later, after a long concert and too much cake, my host father quizzed me about the Holy Ghost, offered to speak in tongues, to teach me to speak in tongues; as if I too were a doll in need of filling.

Vase

As snow fell, the thrift-store filled. Amish girls disguised as old women in Alfred Dunner sweaters cluck over their customers. The vase, white floral-and-bamboo china named after some dynasty, is a lonely object of beauty. A village will do that to you. The German dialect my sister and I speak *one side*, the pair of jeans I hold longingly *the other side*. I buy the vase for what it can hold.

Apple Core

After Christmas, Mom and I brought home some white Lido Beach sand, as if to remind ourselves that the small, dry bodies of dead creatures make beauty, too. We piled the family's shell collection in a prominent place of coming-and-going: on the desk with the glass top and small gold lamp, close to the shoes and coats, where we eat apples in a hurry, and sometimes prop the cores up against this tableau as if to say: *we are dying, we are lovely.*

Whisky and Merton in the Country of Spring

> *We weep for love*
> *in the imperfect wood*
> *in the land of bodies*
>
> —Thomas Merton, "May Song"

Between the chapel and infirmary
I thought I heard a goose,
looked up for the body and saw

only the American flag, it's snap
like a woman's skirt at the edge of a battlefield.
The joke on me, shiny magnolia

leaves, a stray branch touching high
the wavy pane of old glass, giving a call
so different from the clear wavering

voices of sisters at Mass earlier,
and I, passing under the windows of their prayers
then, unsure of where to go

went to the graveyard to say hello
to the many girls my age from the edge of
the frontier. So encountering

the first tentative forsythia blooms hiding
from winter's last retreating soldiers,
it was like finding their far-off lamps

in a travelled night. I wanted to pick a daffodil
and place it on one of the sister's graves,
but I wanted to do it because I wanted to

and not because it sounded nice.
And so began my week of contemplation:
a shadow following spring around a graveyard

and other winding paths, every sound
a painful truth, or a question like *do you suppose*.

— After Exile: Notes for a Song

When I find the dead bird
in the grass, it's a downy woodpecker
so warm still I can't bear
to touch it, find a bucket to carry it
across the road to the cow-pasture

its wings un-bloodied and perfect
(playing-dead beautiful), as if, pressed
by the hoof of a frisking heifer

a Chopin nocturne might roll
from its breast, like a tiny player-piano

o that country girl!
yelling at a speeding coal truck
gnat-helpless, swearing at the sun
all that and breath, the daisies are
in full swing, she says, this body a boat

on the hill: *what anger?* Something
between a stream and a gushing stream
a road named for abandoned Amish
    farms
the only blue a little blue line now
that echoes mountains, but is fields of
    clover.

W hat we talk about when we talk in June—

These are the days I live for, my mother says,
after twenty-three quarts of applesauce,

soft pink from red peelings. A storm is blowing in,
and we head for the balcony, because *that's a tall order.*

In June, you can spend an hour looking
at all the shapes the light makes; a porcelain cloud

standing over the cow pasture; the thin shade a letter casts
during a break from weeding. I cursed a little—Ok, I cried too,

when I discovered my brother spray-poisoned all the flowers
growing outside the new brick garden wall—

snapdragons and poppies mostly. *He meant well*, Mom says,
bringing me three deviled eggs on a plate. In the evenings she wonders

what her sister-in-law was thinking when she collapsed
into the azalea bush outside her own front door;

three days later at the mortician, her fingernails were still blue,
which means her heart really tried, Mom says, ever the nurse.

On a daily walk, I spot a pair of bluebirds in the cows' shade tree,
the orange trim of their waistcoats tiny sunsets, or ribbons
we drop into the wells of our memory, just to see the ripples.

Baptismal Day

White, as you'd expect, my dress hangs across from Mom's washer and dryer. It has the most careful tucks and stitches, *by hand*, her trademark; the star neck-line and puffy tulip sleeves her way of making it extra-special. How like a child in God's best dandelion field I was that day: playful/sober/playful/sober, all crisped and smoothed, the ribbons of my white bonnet blowing in a breeze heady with azaleas. When I knelt and the water was poured—three times!—some girlish part of me remained untucked: *it's messing up my hair.* (How I hated the short curls, "horns," as the other girls called them, sprouting at my ears.) Afterwards, we sang "O happy day that fixed my choice, on Thee my Savior and my God"; afterwards, the mothers of the church showered me with holy kisses, as if I were a bride. Look at it now, browning and crumpled in the room where we pile our towels and underwear: as if some part of me I could never fully inhabit still clings to it, and I can't go back, no matter the longing.

Something about Defiance—

The body is a helpless gesture in spring,
unwanted letters from a prisoner in Poland
piling up under starry green, the maples
with their gentle look, *leave me alone to dress.*

I'm preparing for another journey back
to the mountains, landscape of first love
stark as a blackbird in a magnolia tree—
youth is lost like that, the sky pretending

and then not pretending. The clearest line
we know, the road home. Sometimes love
isn't enough, little basket for collecting
flowers, then fruit, then—.

When my girl body gave out, I floated
a while, finally realizing the study of pain
is an art form: *how to eat chicken feet, etc.,*
and I in this new silver light its note-taker.

In the hopeful canvas of—

A glass bell,
 just far enough away from a pair of boy-shoes, circa 1920s
 draped with a string of pearls like *I'm sorry.*

My grandfather's, and he would not approve of their beauty in sentimentality.
But then, there are the triple-headed lilacs he left me,
 dazzling only once a year.

I am the frame that holds the memory.
These days, the beds of once dreamy-blue hydrangea and peonies are fertile in
 their dying. I am
weary of love,
 or maybe just weary, the bed *I* rest in each night a girl's canoe
for going down the river. My pillows, oars for dreaming: one
 an unwieldy feathered square from Dresden,
 the other a solid pulling-over-my-ear puff

my grandmother stuffed with real gooses-feathers,
which still carry her voice: *it isn't too late to let the moon be the moon.*

A Song for Wandering—

When the sunflowers sprang up
the day fed itself on seeds and light
carried back and forth by birds of
a certain song. Eyelet of red along
that wing, ring of blue, white cap
in the bush and back. Harmony
like mountain hands at their fiddles
and looms, and now mine: transplanted,
wild for blueberries, a little soft
and unsure of the craft of *longing*
from which my grandmother stitched
the most heart-breaking quilts,
little heavens on which to dream dreams
of plenty. What can I do but imitate
wonder, and shape myself after it.

I owe so many debts of gratitude—:

To my mother, who sang to me before I was born, and whose mental leaps—wondering about Nebuchadnezzar while making cheeseburger soup—have afforded me endless poetic inspiration; but mostly for the love and support she's shown her strange, unicorn child.

To my first poetry teacher, Bob King, who convinced me that a poet can be sturdy, logical and chimerical all at once, and who nurtured the seeds of poetry in me I did not recognize.

To John, for sharing his fish and sheep and peace, and for helping me to always see the light at the end of the tunnel. And to Sarah and Mary Ann, for their endless kindness, and for sharing their big porch in summer, that little slice of heaven.

To the Sisters of Loretto in Nerinx, KY, for providing such a beautiful and welcoming campus for retreatants, where many of these poems came to life.

To my lovely, talented and kind MFA family: Mary Ann Samyn, my thesis advisor and poetry mother, who helped me hone my voice ("write that down") and taught me how to be a poet in the world; to Jim Harms, for his insistence on clarity, and wonderful insights and guidance; to The (original) Poet Girls, Christina Rothenbeck, Danielle

Ryle, and Tori Moore, who made workshops both incredibly playful and productive. And of course to all the poets who helped round out the MFA family: Rachel King, Lisa Beans, Lauren Reed, Melissa Atkinson-Mercer, Micah Holmes, Aaron Rote, Matt London, and Kori Frazier-Morgan.

—With special gratitude to those who read draft-after-draft of *After June* since its inception: Danielle Ryle, Rachel King, and Christina Seymour. Your lovely/loving shadows fall across every poem.

—With special gratitude to Sarah Beth Childers for her invaluable friendship and readership during and after the MFA.

To Vincent, who helped me explore off-the-beaten path beauties of West Virginia, helped me move five times in less than two years (while I was writing this book), and has always believed in my work.

To Amie Whittemore, for selecting my manuscript as the winner of The Hopper Poetry Prize, and to all the wonderful people at Green Writers Press, especially Dede Cummings, for her expert guidance, support and enthusiasm, and Caroline Shea, for her amazing attention to detail and wonderful feedback in the book's final polishing stages.

To Michelle Kingdom, for allowing me to use her stunning piece, "Light as Dust," as my cover art.

To Kristy Bowen and *dancing girl press*, for publishing a selection of these poems in my chapbook, *Girl Escaping with Sky* in 2014.

And finally, to the editors of the following journals, where some of these poems first found homes (at times as slightly different versions):

- *Arts & Letters*: "Mountains, Sunset, Redbird, River"
- *Pennsylvania English*: "I haven't loved too many boys"
- *Rock & Sling*: "That Evening Light I Love," "I Always Want to Look at Art This Way" and "Imagine How Much Beauty You Miss Everyday"
- *Windhover*: "Little Cup of Stars" and *"Benedic Anima"*
- *Moon City Review*: "Conflict is the Only Way to Intimacy," "After June" and "Beauty is a Mountain we See When Driving our Car"
- *Quiddity*: "Why Taking Notes on Vermeer is really a Cover-up for—"
- *The Laurel Review*: "How to Bear With it," "Sharing 'A Song on the End of the World'" and "Landscape after Rain"
- *Relief: A Journal of Art and Faith*: "Complaint, Comply, Compline"
- *The Puritan: Frontiers in New English*: "The Obligation of Human Nature in Miniature"
- *Ruminate*: "The Afterlife of Lepidoptera" (which won second place in the Janet M. McCabe Poetry competition in 2014), "How to say *creature comforts* in winter," and "Walking, with Blackberries"
- *Tahoma Literary Review*: "Every Stargazer Knows Her Vowels"
- *Lightning Key Review*: "My Noon, My Midnight, My Talk, My Song" and "Whiskey and Merton in the Country of Spring"
- *Ink & Letters*: "I'm All Prayed Up"
- *Anthology of Appalachian Writers*, **Frank X Walker Volume VI:** "There's a Black Cat in My Garden"

- *Poetry South*: "Doorways"
- *Rougarou*: "Let's Not be Abstract about This" and "May Elegy"
- *Redivider*: "Of all the houses far from home I've haunted—"
- *Eastern Iowa Review*: "Artifacts"
- *The Kenyon Review*: "Something about Defiance"
- *Zone 3*: "In the hopeful canvas of—"
- *Dappled Things*: "A Song for Wandering"

About the Author—

Charity Gingerich is from Uniontown, OH. She obtained her MFA at West Virginia University, and lived in Morgantown, WV for over six years, where she taught a variety of writing courses at WVU and Fairmont State University. Since returning to Ohio, she has taught literature and creative writing at the University of Mount Union, and currently teaches ESL to international business persons and their families. Her work has appeared in journals such as *FIELD*, the *Kenyon Review*, *Arts & Letters*, *Ruminate*, and *Indiana Review*, among others. When not writing and teaching, she enjoys singing with various choral groups.

About the Artist—

Born and raised in Los Angeles, Michelle Kingdom studied drawing and painting at UCLA, earning a Bachelor's degree in fine art. Quietly creating figurative narratives in thread for years, Michelle is a self-taught embroiderer who now exhibits her work nationally and internationally. Her embroideries have been featured in numerous publications such as *The Huffington Post, Hi Fructose, Juxtapoz, Saatchi Gallery*, and *Colossal*. When not busy stitching, Michelle is a preschool teacher and lives in Burbank, CA with her husband and daughter.